The Housing Fix
Public Housing As
A Controlled Substance

By

Melvin Prince Johnakin

The Housing Fix, Public Housing As A Controlled Substance

Foreword

In "The Housing Fix" we embark on a journey to reimagine the role of public housing in shaping a more equitable and prosperous future for all. This book challenges us to see public housing not as a mere Band-Aid for housing insecurity but as a powerful tool for empowerment, socioeconomic mobility, and wealth creation.

As we stand at a critical juncture in history, facing the urgent challenges of housing affordability, economic inequality, and systemic injustice, the need to transform public housing has never been more pressing. "Public Housing: The Fix" offers a bold vision for the future, one where public housing serves as a platform for social change and community resilience.

Through a combination of visionary ideas, practical strategies, and real-world examples, this book guides us on a path toward building a better future through public housing. It challenges us to think creatively, act boldly, and collaborate effectively to address the complex issues facing our communities.

The author of "The Housing Fix" brings a wealth of expertise and passion to this important topic. Their insights, research, and lived experiences shed light on the transformative potential of public housing as a catalyst for positive change in our society.

As we delve into the pages of this book, let us open our minds to new possibilities, challenge our assumptions, and embrace the power of collective action. Let us commit ourselves to creating a more just, inclusive, and sustainable future where public housing is not just a fix but a foundation for a brighter tomorrow.

I invite you to join me on this inspiring journey through the pages of "The Public Housing Fix." Together, let us explore the transformative power of public housing and envision a world where every individual has the opportunity to thrive and succeed.

Introduction

Public housing stands as a complex and multifaceted institution in modern society, serving as a critical resource for individuals and families in need of affordable housing. However, beneath the surface of this seemingly benevolent system lies a web of intricacies and power dynamics that have far-reaching implications for the very individuals it was designed to support. In this book, we will embark on a journey to uncover the hidden truths behind public housing, examining it through a provocative lens as a controlled substance that perpetuates wealth disparities and inequality among low-income and non-educated populations.

At its core, public housing was conceived with noble intentions – to provide a safety net for those who could not afford market-rate housing, offering a stable foundation upon which individuals could build their lives. Yet, as we delve deeper into the current state of public housing, we are confronted with a stark reality: a system that often traps its inhabitants in cycles of poverty and dependency, rather than serving as a stepping stone towards economic empowerment.

For low-income and non-educated individuals, public housing is not just a place to call home; it is a lifeline, a lifeline that can either uplift or ensnare, depending on the forces at play. The impact of public housing on these vulnerable populations is profound, shaping their opportunities, aspirations, and ultimately, their destinies. By exploring the intricate interplay between public housing and socioeconomic dynamics, we aim to shed light on the ways in which this institution can either empower or disempower those it was meant to serve.

The landscape of public housing today is fraught with complexities, where economic interests, political agendas, and social dynamics converge to shape the lived experiences of millions of individuals across the country. From the dilapidated high-rises of urban centers to the sprawling developments in suburban enclaves, public housing embodies a paradoxical reality – a place of refuge and a site of struggle, a source of stability and a locus of instability.

Through the lens of public housing as a controlled substance, we will interrogate the power dynamics at play within this system, examining how wealth, privilege, and influence intersect to shape the fates of those on the margins of society. By unpacking the hidden mechanisms that govern public housing, we aim to challenge prevailing narratives and spark a conversation about the urgent need for reform and renewal in this critical sector of our social fabric.

Join us on this journey of discovery and revelation as we peel back the layers of public housing to reveal the truths that lie beneath the surface. Together we will confront the uncomfortable realities, unearth the hidden injustices, and envision a future where public housing serves as a vehicle for empowerment, equity, and justice for all.

Chapter 1

The Origins of Public Housing

Public housing in the United States has a complex and multifaceted history, rooted in social, economic, and political dynamics that have evolved over the past century. This chapter will explore the origins of public housing, tracing its development from early 20th-century reforms to its establishment as a federal program. The intent is to provide a comprehensive understanding of why public housing was deemed necessary, how it was implemented, and the socio-cultural impacts it has had on American society.

The concept of public housing in the United States began to take shape in the early 1900s, during a period of rapid urbanization and industrialization. The influx of immigrants and rural Americans into cities created severe housing shortages and led to the development of overcrowded and unsanitary tenement districts. These substandard living conditions were brought to public attention through the efforts of social reformers, journalists, and photographers, most notably Jacob Riis, whose work "How the Other Half Lives" (1890) highlighted the dire conditions in New York City's slums.

In response to these conditions, early housing reforms were initiated by local governments and private philanthropists. One of the first significant efforts was the establishment of model tenements, which aimed to provide better housing for the working poor. These initiatives, however, were limited in scope and failed to meet the growing demand for affordable housing.

The Progressive Era (1890s-1920s) saw increased advocacy for government intervention in housing. Reformers argued that decent housing was a public responsibility and essential for the health, safety, and welfare of urban populations. The passage of the Tenement House Act of 1901 in New York City was a landmark in housing reform, setting minimum standards for light, air, and sanitation in new tenement buildings.

The Great Depression of the 1930s exacerbated housing problems, with widespread unemployment and poverty leading to increased homelessness and the deterioration of existing housing stock. The dire economic conditions created a political climate conducive to federal intervention in housing.

The New Deal, introduced by President Franklin D. Roosevelt, marked a turning point in the federal government's role in housing. The National Industrial Recovery Act (NIRA) of 1933 included provisions for slum clearance and the construction of new housing. This was followed by the establishment of the Public Works Administration (PWA), which funded the construction of public housing projects across the country.

The Housing Act of 1937, also known as the Wagner-Steagall Act, was a pivotal piece of legislation that established the United States Housing Authority (USHA). The USHA was tasked with providing loans to local public housing agencies (PHAs) for the construction and management of low-cost housing. The act aimed to address both the immediate need for affordable housing and the long-term goal of eliminating urban slums.

The outbreak of World War II temporarily halted the expansion of public housing as resources were diverted to the war effort. However, the postwar period saw renewed interest in public housing, driven by the housing shortage faced by returning veterans and the rapid suburbanization of American cities.

The Housing Act of 1949, part of President Harry S. Truman's Fair Deal, aimed to address the postwar housing crisis. The act authorized the construction of 810,000 units of public housing and emphasized slum clearance and urban redevelopment. This period saw the construction of large public housing projects in major cities, such as Pruitt-Igoe in St. Louis and Cabrini-Green in Chicago.

Despite the initial optimism surrounding public housing, the program faced significant challenges and criticisms. The design and management of large public housing projects often led to social isolation and concentrated poverty. Many projects were poorly maintained and became associated with crime and neglect.

Critics argued that public housing policies often reinforced racial segregation. The placement of public housing projects frequently mirrored existing patterns of segregation, and discriminatory practices, such as redlining, limited the housing options available to minority communities. The

Civil Rights Movement of the 1960s brought attention to these issues, leading to calls for more equitable housing policies.

In the latter half of the 20th century, public housing policy underwent significant shifts. The Housing and Urban Development Act of 1965 established the Department of Housing and Urban Development (HUD) and introduced programs aimed at promoting homeownership and private sector involvement in affordable housing.

The 1970s and 1980s saw a move away from large-scale public housing projects towards more decentralized approaches, such as Section 8 vouchers, which provide rental assistance to low-income families in the private market. This shift was driven by the recognition of the limitations and failures of traditional public housing models.

In recent decades, there has been a focus on mixed-income developments and the revitalization of distressed public housing projects through initiatives such as HOPE VI. These initiatives aimed to transform deteriorating public housing into mixed-income communities by leveraging public-private partnerships and involving residents in the redevelopment process. The goal was to create more sustainable and integrated communities, addressing the social and economic issues that had plagued earlier public housing projects.

The original intent of public housing was multifaceted, addressing both immediate and long-term social and economic goals. Key objectives included:

1. **Providing Decent, Safe, and Affordable Housing: ** At its core, public housing aimed to ensure that low-income families had access to housing that met basic standards of decency, safety, and affordability. This was seen as essential for improving public health and reducing social disparities.
2. **Eliminating Slums and Blight: ** Public housing was part of broader urban renewal efforts aimed at clearing slums and revitalizing urban areas. By replacing substandard housing with new developments, policymakers hoped to improve living conditions and stimulate economic development.
3. **Promoting Social Stability and Integration: ** Public housing was

envisioned as a means of promoting social stability by providing secure housing for vulnerable populations, reducing homelessness, and supporting family cohesion. Additionally, there was an aspiration to integrate different social and economic groups, though this goal often proved challenging in practice

4. **Supporting Economic Recovery and Job Creation: ** During the Great Depression and subsequent economic downturns, public housing projects were also seen as a means of stimulating the economy by creating construction jobs and boosting demand for materials and services.

5. **Addressing Racial and Economic Inequities: ** Over time, public housing policies increasingly aimed to address racial and economic inequities in access to housing. This included efforts to combat discrimination and segregation, although the effectiveness of these policies has been a subject of ongoing debate and critique.

Case Studies and Notable Projects

Several public housing projects serve as notable case studies, illustrating both the successes and challenges of public housing in the United States.

1. **Pruitt-Igoe (St. Louis, Missouri):** Initially hailed as a model of modernist architecture and urban planning, Pruitt-Igoe became infamous for its rapid decline and eventual demolition in the 1970s. The failure of Pruitt-Igoe highlighted the limitations of high-density, high-rise public housing and the importance of social and management factors in the success of housing projects.

2. **Cabrini-Green (Chicago, Illinois):** Another iconic public housing project, Cabrini-Green experienced severe social and economic challenges, including crime and neglect. Efforts to redevelop Cabrini-Green into a mixed-income community have been part of broader strategies to address the failures of traditional public housing.

3. **Harlem River Houses (New York City, New York):** One of the first public

housing projects funded by the federal
government, the Harlem River Houses
aimed to provide quality housing for African
American families during the New Deal era.
Despite facing challenges, the project is
often cited as a more successful example of
early public housing, partly due to its
smaller scale and community-focused
design.

The history of public housing in the United States
offers several key lessons for future housing
policy:

1. **Importance of Design and Community
    Engagement:** The design and scale of
    public housing projects significantly impact
    their success. Smaller, community-oriented
    developments tend to fare better than large,
    impersonal high-rises. Engaging residents in
    the planning and management of housing
    projects can also improve outcomes.

2. **Need for Comprehensive Support
    Services:** Housing alone is not sufficient
    to address the needs of low-income families.
    Comprehensive support services, including
    education, employment, and healthcare, are

essential for fostering stable and thriving communities.

3. **Addressing Systemic Inequities:** Effective public housing policy must address systemic inequities, including racial segregation and economic disparities. This requires not only equitable housing policies but also broader social and economic reforms.

4. **Flexibility and Innovation:** Public housing programs must be flexible and adaptable to changing social and economic conditions. Innovative approaches, such as public-private partnerships and mixed-income developments, can help create more sustainable and inclusive housing solutions.

The origins of public housing in the United States reflect a complex interplay of social, economic, and political factors. From early reform efforts to federal initiatives under the New Deal and beyond, public housing has aimed to provide decent, affordable housing for those in need while addressing broader urban challenges. Despite significant challenges and criticisms, public housing remains a crucial component of the nation's housing policy. By learning from past experiences and embracing innovative approaches, policymakers can continue to work towards the goal of ensuring safe, affordable, and inclusive housing for all Americans. How public housing was meant to provide affordable housing for those in need.

Chapter 2

The Evolution of Public Housing Policies

Public housing policies have undergone significant transformations since their inception, reflecting broader societal changes and evolving understandings of poverty, urban development, and social welfare. These policies, initially rooted in the early 20th century's progressive ideals, have shifted through various phases, each with distinct characteristics and implications for low-income individuals. This chapter delves into the historical trajectory of public housing policies, exploring key milestones, policy shifts, and their impacts on low-income populations.

The Early Foundations: 1930s to 1940s

The genesis of public housing in the United States can be traced back to the Great Depression era, a time when economic hardship and unemployment were rampant. The Federal Housing Act of 1937 marked a watershed moment, establishing the United States Housing Authority (USHA). This act was predicated on the belief that safe, affordable housing was a fundamental right and a public responsibility.

Early public housing projects were characterized by their focus on urban renewal and slum clearance. The aim was to replace dilapidated, overcrowded tenements with modern, hygienic housing. These early developments, such as those in New York City and Chicago, were often stark, utilitarian structures. While they provided much-needed housing, they also set a precedent for segregated and isolated communities, inadvertently sowing the seeds for future social challenges.

Post-War Expansion and Redefinition: 1950s to 1960s

The post-World War II era saw a significant expansion of public housing, driven by the housing shortage faced by returning veterans and the burgeoning population. The housing Act of 1949 played a crucial role in this expansion, aiming to provide "a decent home and suitable living environment for every American family."

During this period, public housing began to take on a new character. The focus shifted from mere provision of shelter to the creation of communities. Projects like Pruitt-Igoe in St. Louis, initially hailed as a modernist triumph, exemplified the era's ambition. However, these projects soon fell into disrepair, plagued by poor maintenance, inadequate funding, and social isolation. The failures of such projects highlighted the complexities of public housing and hinted at the need for more nuanced approaches.

The Era of Deconstruction: 1970s to 1980s

By the 1970s, the weaknesses of large-scale public housing projects had become evident. High-rise developments, once symbols of progress, were now seen as failures, breeding grounds for crime and poverty. The demolition of Pruitt-Igoe in 1972 symbolized the broader disillusionment with high-density public housing.

In response, public housing policy began to shift towards deconstruction and decentralization. The Housing and Community Development Act of 1974 introduced the Section 8 program, which provided housing vouchers to low-income families. This marked a significant departure from previous models, emphasizing private market solutions and tenant choice. The shift towards vouchers aimed to integrate low-income families into broader communities, reducing the stigma and segregation associated with traditional public housing.

The Rise of Neoliberalism and Market-Based Solutions: 1980s to 1990s

The 1980s and 1990s witnessed a further shift towards market-based solutions, influenced by the broader neoliberal turn in economic policy. The Reagan administration's cuts to federal housing budgets and the emphasis on privatization reflected a belief in the superiority of market mechanisms over government intervention.

The HOPE VI program, initiated in 1992, epitomized this new approach. It aimed to revitalize distressed public housing through mixed-income developments and public-private partnerships. HOPE VI sought to deconcentrate poverty, promote social integration, and leverage private investment. While the program had successes, it also faced criticism for displacing low-income residents and reducing the overall stock of affordable housing.

The 21ˢᵗ Century: Towards a Holistic Approach

The turn of the 21st century brought a more holistic understanding of public housing, recognizing the need for comprehensive support systems beyond mere shelter. Policies began to emphasize supportive services, community development, and resident empowerment.

The Quality Housing and Work Responsibility Act of 1998, for instance, sought to improve the quality of public housing and promote self-sufficiency among residents. Programs focusing on job training, education, and health services became integral components of public housing initiatives.

Moreover, the concept of "housing first" gained traction. This approach posits that stable housing is a prerequisite for addressing other social issues such as unemployment, mental health, and substance abuse. Programs inspired by the housing first model, such as those targeting homelessness, have shown promising results in improving housing stability and overall well-being.

The Impact on Low-Income Individuals

The evolution of public housing policies has had profound impacts on low-income individuals, both positive and negative. Early public housing projects provided much-needed relief from squalid living conditions but often entrenched segregation and social isolation. The shift towards vouchers and market-based solutions offered greater flexibility and opportunities for integration but also introduced new challenges, such as the limited availability of affordable housing in desirable neighborhoods and the complexities of navigating the private rental market.

Positive Impacts:

1. Improved Living Conditions: Early public housing efforts succeeded in replacing unsafe, overcrowded tenements with safer, more sanitary living environments. This had a significant positive impact on the health and well-being of many low-income families.

2. Increased Access to Housing: Programs like Section 8 vouchers expanded housing options for low-income families, allowing

them to choose housing in various neighborhoods rather than being confined to public housing projects. This increased access to better schools, job opportunities, and safer environments.

3. Community Revitalization: Mixed-income developments under programs like HOPE VI aimed to revitalize distressed neighborhoods by attracting a diverse socio-economic population. This often led to improved community amenities, reduced crime rates, and enhanced social cohesion.

4. Supportive Services: The integration of supportive services in public housing policies, such as job training and healthcare, has helped residents achieve greater stability and self-sufficiency. Programs that adopt a holistic approach recognize that housing is just one piece of a larger puzzle in addressing poverty.

Negative Impacts:

1. **Displacement**: The demolition of large
    public housing projects and the shift towards
    mixed-income developments often resulted
    in the displacement of low-income residents.
    Many former residents were unable to return
    to their neighborhoods due to higher rents or
    a lack of affordable units, exacerbating
    housing insecurity.

2. **Market Limitations**: While housing
    vouchers increased choice, the reality of the
    private rental market posed challenges.
    Landlords in desirable neighborhoods might
    refuse vouchers, discriminate against
    voucher holders, or charge rents beyond the
    voucher limits, leaving many low-income
    families with limited options.

3. **Segregation and Isolation**: Early public
    housing projects often reinforced racial and
    economic segregation by concentrating
    poverty in specific areas. Even with later
    policies aimed at deconcentration, many
    low-income individuals continued to face
    social and geographic isolation.

4. **Inadequate Funding and Maintenance**:
   Chronic underfunding of public housing has
   led to deteriorating conditions in many
   developments. Maintenance backlogs, safety
   issues, and insufficient resources have
   plagued public housing authorities, affecting
   the quality of life for residents.

5. **Stigma**: Public housing and its
   residents have often been stigmatized, seen
   as symbols of failure rather than as essential
   components of the social safety net. This
   stigma has perpetuated negative stereotypes
   and hindered efforts to create inclusive,
   supportive communities.

Emphasis on Sustainability and Resilience:

Modern public housing policies are increasingly
focusing on sustainability and resilience,
recognizing the need to build housing that can
withstand environmental challenges and reduce
carbon footprints. Incorporating green building
practices, energy efficiency, and climate resilience
into public housing can improve living conditions
and reduce long-term costs.

Technology Integration:

Advancements in technology offer new opportunities for public housing. Smart home technologies can improve safety, reduce energy consumption, and enhance the quality of life for residents. Additionally, digital tools can streamline the management of housing programs, making it easier for residents to access services and for authorities to monitor and maintain housing stock.

Greater Resident Involvement:

Empowering residents to have a say in the design, management, and governance of their housing communities is crucial. Resident councils, participatory budgeting, and community-led initiatives can ensure that housing policies are responsive to the needs and aspirations of those they serve.

Comprehensive Support Systems:

Recognizing that housing alone does not solve poverty, future policies must integrate comprehensive support systems, including education, healthcare, employment training, and mental health services. A holistic approach addresses the interconnected challenges faced by low-income individuals, promoting stability and upward mobility.

Inclusion and Equity:

Ensuring that public housing policies promote inclusion and equity is vital. This involves addressing systemic inequalities, eliminating discrimination, and creating opportunities for all residents, regardless of race, gender, or socioeconomic status. Policies should aim to create diverse, vibrant communities where everyone can thrive.

Innovative Financing Models:

To address funding challenges, innovative financing models are needed. Public-private partnerships, social impact bonds, and community land trusts are examples of approaches that can leverage additional resources and create sustainable, affordable housing solutions.

The evolution of public housing policies reflects a complex interplay of social, economic, and political forces. From the early days of slum clearance and urban renewal to the modern focus on sustainability and comprehensive support systems, each phase has brought new insights and challenges. The impact on low-income individuals has been profound, with public housing serving as both a lifeline and a source of contention.

As we move forward, it is essential to learn from past experiences, embrace innovative solutions, and maintain a steadfast commitment to ensuring that everyone has access to safe, affordable, and dignified housing. Public housing policies must continue to evolve, guided by principles of equity, inclusion, and sustainability, to create communities where all individuals can achieve their full potential.

The Role of Grassroots Movements and Advocacy:

An often overlooked but critical component in the evolution of public housing policies is the role played by grassroots movements and advocacy groups. Throughout history, residents and community organizations have been instrumental in pushing for reforms and holding policymakers accountable. Their efforts have ensured that the voices of those most affected by housing policies are heard.

Early Advocacy and Tenant Movements:

In the early days of public housing, tenant movements emerged as powerful forces for change. Organizations like the National Tenants Organization (NTO), founded in the 1960s, advocated for the rights of public housing residents, fighting against poor living conditions, rent increases, and evictions. These movements brought to light the everyday struggles of low-income families and pushed for more humane and just housing policies.

The Role of Civil Rights Activism:

The civil rights movement of the 1960s and 1970s significantly influenced public housing policies, highlighting the intersections between race, poverty, and housing. Activists and organizations, such as the NAACP and the Southern Christian Leadership Conference (SCLC), campaigned against discriminatory housing practices and segregation. Their efforts led to landmark legislation, such as the Fair Housing Act of 1968, which aimed to eliminate racial discrimination in housing.

Modern Advocacy and Policy Reform:

In contemporary times, advocacy groups continue to play a crucial role in shaping public housing policies. Organizations like the National Low Income Housing Coalition (NLIHC) work tirelessly to advocate for affordable housing, influence legislation, and provide resources for low-income residents. These groups use research, policy analysis, and grassroots mobilization to push for systemic changes that benefit low-income communities.

International Perspectives on Public Housing:

While this chapter primarily focuses on the evolution of public housing policies in the United States, it is important to consider international perspectives. Different countries have adopted various models and approaches to public housing, offering valuable lessons and insights.

The European Approach:

Many European countries have a long tradition of social housing, with significant government investment in affordable housing. Countries like the Netherlands and Sweden have extensive social housing programs that provide high-quality, mixed-income housing. These models emphasize the integration of affordable housing within communities, reducing stigma and promoting social cohesion.

The Singapore Model:

Singapore's public housing policy is often cited as a success story. The Housing and Development Board (HDB) has provided affordable, high-quality housing to the majority of the population. The HDB's approach focuses on homeownership, with various schemes to help residents purchase their flats. This model has fostered a sense of community and stability, contributing to Singapore's social and economic development.

Challenges and Innovations in Developing Countries:

In developing countries, public housing faces unique challenges, including rapid urbanization, limited resources, and informal settlements. Innovative solutions, such as community-led housing initiatives and incremental housing approaches, have emerged to address these challenges. For instance, the Favela-Bairro project in Rio de Janeiro, Brazil, focuses on upgrading informal settlements, providing infrastructure, and integrating them into the urban fabric.

The Future of Public Housing Policies

Looking ahead, the future of public housing policies will likely be shaped by several key trends and challenges:

Climate Change and Environmental Sustainability

As the impacts of climate change become more pronounced, public housing policies must prioritize environmental sustainability. This includes building energy-efficient homes, incorporating green spaces, and ensuring that housing is resilient to climate-related disasters.

Sustainable housing not only reduces environmental impact but also lowers utility costs for residents, contributing to long-term affordability.

Technological Advancements

Advancements in technology offer new opportunities to improve public housing. Smart home technologies can enhance safety, convenience, and energy efficiency. Digital platforms can streamline tenant services, making it easier for residents to access resources and for housing authorities to manage properties. Embracing technology can lead to more responsive and efficient public housing systems.

Addressing Systemic Inequalities

Future public housing policies must address systemic inequalities that have historically marginalized certain groups. This includes ensuring equitable access to housing for racial and ethnic minorities, people with disabilities, and other vulnerable populations. Policies should focus on eliminating discrimination, promoting inclusion, and creating opportunities for all residents to thrive.

Holistic Community Development

Recognizing that housing is interconnected with other aspects of life, future policies should adopt a holistic approach to community development. This involves integrating housing with education, healthcare, transportation, and employment opportunities. By creating comprehensive support systems, public housing can serve as a foundation for broader social and economic development.

Innovative Financing and Partnerships

Securing adequate funding for public housing remains a critical challenge. Innovative financing models, such as social impact bonds and public-private partnerships, can help leverage additional resources. Collaborations between government, private sector, and non-profit organizations can lead to creative solutions that expand affordable housing options.

Empowering Residents

Empowering residents to take an active role in their communities is essential for the success of public housing policies. This includes involving residents in decision-making processes, supporting tenant associations, and fostering a sense of ownership and community engagement. When residents have a stake in their housing and community, they are more likely to contribute to its upkeep and improvement.

Global Collaboration and Knowledge Sharing

As countries around the world grapple with similar housing challenges, international collaboration and knowledge sharing can play a crucial role in shaping effective public housing policies. Platforms for exchanging best practices, research, and innovations can help policymakers learn from global experiences and tailor solutions to their unique contexts.

The evolution of public housing policies is a testament to society's ongoing struggle to provide safe, affordable, and dignified housing for all. From the early days of slum clearance and urban renewal to modern approaches emphasizing sustainability, equity, and comprehensive support systems, each phase has brought valuable lessons and new challenges.

For low-income individuals, public housing has been both a lifeline and a source of contention. While it has provided essential shelter and opportunities for many, it has also faced criticism for segregation, displacement, and inadequate funding. The future of public housing depends on our ability to learn from past experiences, embrace innovative solutions, and maintain a steadfast commitment to equity, inclusion, and sustainability.

Policymakers, advocates, and communities must work together to ensure that public housing evolves to meet the needs of the 21st century. By prioritizing environmental sustainability, leveraging technological advancements, addressing systemic inequalities, and fostering holistic community development, we can create public housing policies that not only provide shelter but also empower individuals and strengthen communities.

As we move forward, it is essential to recognize the role of grassroots movements and advocacy in shaping public housing policies. These efforts have been instrumental in pushing for reforms and ensuring that the voices of those most affected by housing policies are heard. By continuing to involve residents in decision-making processes and supporting their active participation in their communities, we can build more resilient, inclusive, and vibrant neighborhoods.

In conclusion, the journey of public housing policies reflects a broader societal commitment to social justice and equity. While challenges remain, the ongoing evolution of these policies offers hope for a future where everyone has access to safe, affordable, and dignified housing. By embracing innovative solutions, fostering collaboration, and prioritizing the needs and rights of low-income individuals, public housing can serve as a cornerstone for building stronger, more inclusive communities.

Government Interventions and Their Effects on Public Housing Programs

Government interventions play a crucial role in shaping public housing programs around the world. This essay explores various government

interventions and their effects on public housing
initiatives. By examining different approaches
taken by governments, we can gain insights into
the impact of these interventions on the success
and sustainability of public housing programs.

Public housing programs are essential for
providing affordable housing to low-income
individuals and families. Governments worldwide
have implemented various interventions to address
housing shortages, homelessness, and urban
development challenges. These interventions range
from direct provision of housing to financial
incentives for private developers. In this essay, we
will explore the effects of government
interventions on public housing programs,
considering both the positive outcomes and
challenges associated with these initiatives.

**Government Interventions in Public Housing
Programs:**

1. **Direct Provision of Public Housing:**
   One of the most common government
   interventions is the direct provision of public
   housing units. Governments build and
   manage housing complexes to offer

affordable accommodation to low-income residents. While this intervention addresses the immediate need for housing, challenges such as maintenance costs, social stigma, and concentration of poverty can arise.

2. **Subsidies and Vouchers:** Governments often provide subsidies or vouchers to low-income individuals to help them afford housing in the private market. These interventions aim to increase housing choice and promote socioeconomic integration. However, limited funding, eligibility criteria, and market fluctuations can affect the effectiveness of these programs.

3. **Rent Control and Regulations:** Rent control policies set limits on rent increases to protect tenants from excessive price hikes. While these regulations can make housing more affordable for some residents, they may also discourage investment in rental properties and lead to supply shortages in the long run.

4. **Mixed-Income and Inclusionary Zoning:** Some governments implement policies that require developers to include affordable housing units in mixed-income developments. Inclusionary zoning aims to create diverse communities and prevent segregation based on income. However, challenges such as opposition from developers and neighborhood resistance can hinder the implementation of these policies.

5. **Public-Private Partnerships:** Collaborations between the government and private sector have become increasingly common in public housing initiatives. These partnerships leverage private sector expertise and resources to develop affordable housing projects. While PPPs can expedite project delivery and improve efficiency, concerns about transparency, accountability, and profit motives have been raised.

Effects of Government Interventions on Public Housing Programs:

1. **Access to Affordable Housing:**
    Government interventions play a crucial role
    in expanding access to affordable housing
    for low-income individuals and families.
    Subsidies, vouchers, and public housing
    units help address housing affordability
    challenges and reduce homelessness rates.

2. **Social and Economic Integration:**
    Interventions such as mixed-income
    developments and inclusionary zoning
    promote social and economic integration by
    creating diverse communities. These
    initiatives can reduce segregation and
    enhance social cohesion among residents
    from different socioeconomic backgrounds.

3. **Quality of Housing:** Government
    interventions influence the quality of public
    housing units and the maintenance of these
    properties. Adequate funding, regulations,
    and oversight mechanisms are essential to
    ensure that public housing remains safe,
    habitable, and sustainable for residents.

4. **Urban Development and Neighborhood
    Revitalization:** Public housing programs

can contribute to urban development and neighborhood revitalization efforts. Well-designed housing projects can stimulate economic growth, attract investment, and improve the overall livability of communities.

5. **Challenges and Limitations:** Despite their potential benefits, government interventions in public housing programs face several challenges and limitations that can impact their effectiveness:

6. **Funding Constraints:** Limited financial resources can constrain the scale and impact of public housing programs. Governments may struggle to allocate sufficient funding for the construction, maintenance, and operation of public housing units, leading to inadequate housing supply and quality.

7. Bureaucratic Inefficiencies: Government bureaucracies involved in public housing programs may face inefficiencies, red tape, and delays in decision-making processes. These inefficiencies can hinder the timely

delivery of housing projects and reduce the overall effectiveness of interventions.

Stigmatization and NIMBYism:
Public housing developments are sometimes stigmatized by surrounding communities, leading to NIMBY (Not In My Backyard) opposition. Resistance from residents and local authorities can impede the implementation of public housing initiatives and perpetuate social segregation.

Market Forces and Housing Market Dynamics:
Government interventions in the housing market can influence supply and demand dynamics, sometimes leading to unintended consequences. Rent control policies, for example, may distort market incentives and discourage investment in rental properties, affecting housing affordability and availability.

Sustainability and Long-Term Viability:
Ensuring the sustainability and long-term viability of public housing programs is crucial for their success. Governments must

address issues such as maintenance, social services, community engagement, and financial sustainability to create resilient and thriving public housing communities.

Case Studies:

Singapore's Public Housing Program (HDB): The Housing Development Board (HDB) in Singapore is known for its successful public housing program, which provides affordable and quality housing for the majority of the population. Government interventions such as subsidies, public-private partnerships, and strict regulations have contributed to the success of the HDB program.

Housing Choice Voucher Program (Section 8, USA): The Housing Choice Voucher Program, also known as Section 8 in the United States, provides rental assistance to low-income individuals and families. While the program has helped many households afford housing in the private market, challenges such as limited funding, administrative complexities, and landlord participation remain.

Government interventions play a crucial role in shaping public housing programs and addressing housing challenges faced by low-income individuals and families. By implementing a combination of policies, subsidies, regulations, and partnerships, governments can expand access to affordable housing, promote social integration, and contribute to urban development. However, challenges such as funding constraints, bureaucratic inefficiencies, and market dynamics must be carefully addressed to ensure the effectiveness and sustainability of public housing initiatives. Continuous evaluation, stakeholder engagement, and innovation are essential to improve public housing programs and create thriving communities for all residents.

Chapter 3

The Business of Public Housing

Public housing programs involve a complex interplay of economic interests and stakeholders, ranging from government agencies and developers to residents and community organizations. Understanding the business aspects of public housing is essential for analyzing the incentives, challenges, and dynamics that shape the development and management of affordable housing initiatives. In this chapter, we will delve into the economic interests and stakeholders involved in public housing developments, highlighting their roles, motivations, and interactions within the housing ecosystem.

Economic Interests in Public Housing:

1. **Government Entities:** Government agencies at the local, regional, and national levels play a central role in public housing development. These entities allocate funding, set policies, regulate housing

markets, and oversee the implementation of housing programs. Their primary interest lies in addressing housing affordability, social welfare, and urban development goals through targeted interventions and investments.

2. **Real Estate Developers:** Private developers are key players in public housing initiatives, often engaging in public-private partnerships or government contracts to build affordable housing projects. Developers seek opportunities to secure land, obtain financing, navigate regulatory requirements, and manage construction processes to deliver housing units within budget and schedule constraints. Their economic interests include profit generation, market competitiveness, and reputational considerations in the affordable housing sector.

3. **Financial Institutions:** Banks, investors, and financial institutions provide capital for public housing developments through loans, grants, tax credits, and other financial instruments. These entities assess the

financial viability, risk profiles, and return on investment of affordable housing projects to support their economic interests in generating revenue, managing risk exposure, and fulfilling social responsibility objectives.

4. **Nonprofit Organizations:** Nonprofit entities, such as community development corporations (CDCs) and housing advocacy groups, play a vital role in public housing by advocating for affordable housing policies, providing supportive services to residents, and developing community-based initiatives. Their economic interests include promoting social equity, fostering community empowerment, and leveraging resources for sustainable housing solutions.

5. **Residents and Tenants:** Low-income residents and tenants are essential stakeholders in public housing programs, as they are the end-users of affordable housing units. Their economic interests revolve around accessing safe, affordable housing, maintaining housing stability, and participating in decision-making processes

that affect their living conditions. Residents may also advocate for tenant rights, social services, and community amenities to enhance their quality of life.

Stakeholders in Public Housing Developments:

Government Agencies: Local housing authorities, urban planning departments, and housing ministries are primary stakeholders in public housing developments. These entities set policies, allocate funding, issue permits, and monitor compliance with housing standards to ensure the success and sustainability of affordable housing initiatives.

Real Estate Developers: Private developers, including for-profit and non-profit entities, are key stakeholders in public housing projects. Developers acquire land, design housing units, secure financing, manage construction, and oversee property management to deliver affordable housing solutions that meet regulatory requirements and market demands.

Financial Institutions: Banks, investment firms, and philanthropic organizations are critical stakeholders in public housing developments, providing funding, loans, tax incentives, and financial expertise to support affordable housing initiatives. Financial institutions assess project feasibility, manage financial risk, and facilitate capital flows to enable the implementation of affordable housing projects.

Community Organizations: Local community groups, neighborhood associations, and housing nonprofits are important stakeholders in public housing developments. These organizations engage with residents, advocate for community needs, provide social services, and promote community participation in public housing planning and decision-making processes. Community organizations collaborate with developers, government agencies, and residents to ensure that public housing projects align with community priorities and benefit all stakeholders.

Construction and Maintenance Contractors: Construction firms, property management companies, and maintenance contractors are key stakeholders in public housing developments. These entities are responsible for building, repairing, and maintaining affordable housing units to ensure that they meet quality standards, safety regulations, and resident needs. Construction and maintenance contractors play a critical role in the successful implementation and long-term sustainability of public housing projects.

Elected Officials and Policymakers:** Political leaders, elected officials, and policymakers are influential stakeholders in public housing programs. These individuals shape housing policies, allocate resources, enact legislation, and make decisions that impact the design, funding, and governance of affordable housing initiatives. Elected officials and policymakers represent the interests of constituents, advocate for housing equity, and drive systemic changes to address housing challenges within their jurisdictions.

Collaboration and Partnerships: Stakeholders in public housing developments often collaborate and form partnerships to leverage their expertise, resources, and networks. Public-private partnerships, community development collaborations, and joint ventures between developers, government agencies, and nonprofit organizations are common strategies to address complex housing challenges and achieve shared goals in affordable housing initiatives.

Negotiation and Conflict Resolution:** Stakeholders may engage in negotiations and conflict resolution processes to address competing interests, resolve disputes, and find mutually acceptable solutions in public housing projects. Negotiating affordable housing terms, addressing community concerns, and reconciling divergent viewpoints are essential for building consensus, fostering trust, and advancing shared objectives among stakeholders.

Community Engagement and Participation:** Stakeholders actively engage with residents, community organizations, and advocacy groups to promote community participation, gather feedback, and incorporate local perspectives in public housing planning and decision-making processes. Meaningful community engagement enhances transparency, accountability, and social cohesion in public housing developments, fostering a sense of ownership and empowerment among stakeholders.

Data Sharing and Transparency:** Stakeholders exchange information, data, and insights to inform decision-making, monitor project progress, and evaluate the impact of public housing initiatives. Transparent communication, data sharing platforms, and performance metrics help stakeholders track outcomes, assess effectiveness, and adjust strategies to optimize the economic, social, and environmental outcomes of affordable housing projects.

The business of public housing involves a diverse array of economic interests and stakeholders, each playing a unique role in shaping the development, implementation, and management of affordable housing initiatives. By understanding the motivations, interactions, and dynamics among stakeholders, policymakers, developers, residents, and community organizations can collaborate effectively to address housing challenges, promote social equity, and create thriving communities for all. Strong partnerships, community engagement, data-driven decision-making, and transparent communication are essential for fostering inclusive, sustainable, and successful public housing developments that benefit individuals, families, and neighborhoods in need of affordable housing solutions.

Chapter 4

The Illusion of Choice

In the labyrinth of modern urban life, the concept of choice is often heralded as a fundamental pillar of freedom and autonomy. However, for low-income individuals, particularly when it comes to housing, the notion of choice is more illusory than real. This chapter delves into the myriad constraints that render the options for affordable housing limited and often inadequate, thereby perpetuating a cycle of poverty and instability.

The Economic Constraints:

The primary barrier to housing choice for low-income individuals is, unsurprisingly, economic. With limited financial resources, the range of available housing options is severely restricted. Unlike their wealthier counterparts, low-income families cannot afford to prioritize factors such as neighborhood safety, proximity to good schools, or access to public transportation. Instead, they are often forced to select from a narrow band of options that fit within their budget, which are typically in less desirable areas with fewer amenities and higher crime rates.

The disparity in housing costs versus income levels is stark. In many urban areas, the cost of rent for even a modest apartment can consume over half of a low-income family's monthly earnings. This leaves little room for other essential expenses like food, healthcare, and education. The result is a precarious existence where any unexpected expense or loss of income can lead to eviction and homelessness.

The Quality of Available Housing:

The quality of housing available to low-income individuals is another significant issue. Affordable housing units are frequently older and poorly maintained. Problems such as mold, lead paint, faulty plumbing, and inadequate heating and cooling systems are common. These substandard living conditions can have severe health implications, particularly for children and the elderly, who are more vulnerable to environmental hazards.

Moreover, landlords of low-cost housing units often have little incentive to improve their properties. Due to high demand and low supply, they can fill vacancies quickly, even if the units are in poor condition. This dynamic leaves tenants with limited recourse; they can either endure the subpar living conditions or face the daunting task of finding alternative affordable housing.

Geographic and Racial Segregation:

Geographic and racial segregation further exacerbate the illusion of choice. Historically, discriminatory practices like redlining and restrictive covenants have confined low-income and minority groups to specific neighborhoods. Despite legal advancements, the legacy of these practices persists. Low-income housing is overwhelmingly concentrated in certain areas, often far removed from economic opportunities and essential services.

This segregation reinforces a cycle of poverty. Children growing up in these neighborhoods have less access to quality education and are more likely to encounter violence and crime. Furthermore, the lack of nearby job opportunities forces residents to commute long distances, increasing transportation costs and reducing time available for family and community activities.

The Role of Public Policy:

Public policy plays a crucial role in shaping the housing landscape, yet it often falls short of addressing the needs of low-income individuals. Housing assistance programs, such as Section 8 vouchers in the United States, aim to provide relief but are often underfunded and oversubscribed. Many eligible families languish on waiting lists for years, during which time their housing situation remains unstable.

Zoning laws and land use regulations also impact housing availability. In many cities, restrictive zoning laws limit the construction of affordable housing units, effectively pricing low-income families out of certain neighborhoods. These laws often serve the interests of wealthier residents who oppose the development of low-income housing in their communities, citing concerns about property values and neighborhood character.

The Psychological Impact:

The illusion of choice in housing has profound psychological effects on low-income individuals and families. The constant stress of securing and maintaining affordable housing can lead to chronic anxiety and depression. The uncertainty of housing stability creates a pervasive sense of insecurity, making it difficult for individuals to focus on long-term goals and personal development.

Children in these situations are particularly affected. Frequent moves and unstable living conditions disrupt their education and social development. Instability can lead to behavioral problems and academic underachievement, perpetuating the cycle of poverty into the next generation.

Potential Solutions:

Addressing the illusion of choice in housing for low-income individuals requires a multifaceted approach. Increasing the availability of affordable housing is paramount. This can be achieved through a combination of public and private initiatives, including the construction of new affordable housing units, subsidies for low-income renters, and incentives for developers to include affordable units in their projects.

Reforming zoning laws to allow for more diverse housing options in various neighborhoods is also crucial. This can help to integrate low-income families into more affluent areas, providing greater access to quality schools, jobs, and services.

In addition to these structural changes, improving the enforcement of housing quality standards is essential. Ensuring that all rental properties meet basic health and safety requirements can help to mitigate the negative health impacts associated with substandard housing.

Enhanced funding for housing assistance programs is another critical component. Reducing the backlog of applicants and increasing the amount of assistance provided can help more families achieve housing stability.

Finally, addressing the psychological impact of housing insecurity involves providing supportive services to low-income individuals and families. This can include mental health services.

By addressing the broader needs of low-income families, these services can help to break the cycle of poverty and provide a pathway to stability and self-sufficiency.

The Role of Community and Non-Profit Organizations:

Community and non-profit organizations play a vital role in addressing the housing needs of low-income individuals. These organizations often provide essential services such as emergency housing, legal assistance, and advocacy for tenant rights. They also work to create and maintain affordable housing through various initiatives, such as community land trusts and housing cooperatives.

Community land trusts (CLTs) are a particularly innovative solution. CLTs involve the community owning the land while individuals own the homes on that land. This model ensures that the land remains affordable for future generations and prevents speculative increases in property prices. Housing cooperatives, where residents collectively own and manage their housing, can also provide a more stable and affordable option for low-income families.

Technology and Innovation:

Technology and innovation can also play a role in expanding housing choices for low-income individuals. Digital platforms that connect renters with available housing, provide transparency around housing quality, and facilitate communication between tenants and landlords can help to streamline the search process and improve tenant experiences. Additionally, advancements in construction technology, such as modular housing and 3D-printed homes, have the potential to reduce construction costs and increase the supply of affordable housing.

Collaboration and Advocacy:

Addressing the illusion of choice in housing requires collaboration across multiple sectors, including government, private industry, non-profits, and communities. Advocacy for policy changes at the local, state, and federal levels is crucial to creating a more equitable housing landscape. This includes lobbying for increased funding for affordable housing, reforming zoning laws, and ensuring fair housing practices.

Public awareness campaigns can also play a significant role in changing perceptions and garnering support for affordable housing initiatives. By highlighting the stories and struggles of low-income individuals and families, these campaigns can build empathy and drive action towards more inclusive housing policies.

The illusion of choice in housing for low-income individuals is a complex and multifaceted issue. Economic constraints, substandard housing quality, geographic and racial segregation, inadequate public policy, and the psychological toll all contribute to a reality where the options for affordable housing are severely limited. To address this issue, a comprehensive approach is needed that includes increasing the supply of affordable housing, reforming zoning laws, improving housing quality standards, enhancing funding for assistance programs, providing supportive services, and leveraging technology and innovation.

Ultimately, ensuring that low-income individuals have genuine choices in housing is not just a matter of economic necessity but a fundamental issue of social justice. By working together across sectors and advocating for meaningful policy changes, we can create a housing landscape where everyone has the opportunity to live in safe, stable, and affordable homes. Only then can we begin to dismantle the illusion of choice and build a more equitable society.

Public housing, intended to provide affordable shelter for low-income individuals and families, can inadvertently perpetuate cycles of poverty and dependency due to various systemic factors and challenges. While public housing programs aim to offer a safety net for vulnerable populations, they often fall short in addressing the underlying issues that contribute to poverty. In this essay, we will explore how public housing can perpetuate cycles of poverty and dependency, considering factors such as segregation, stigmatization, lack of resources, and limited opportunities for upward mobility.

One of the key ways in which public housing can perpetuate cycles of poverty is through the concentration of poverty in specific neighborhoods. Public housing developments are often clustered together in low-income areas, leading to the creation of economically segregated communities. This concentration of poverty can isolate residents from opportunities for social and economic mobility, as they are surrounded by limited resources and face higher levels of crime, unemployment, and inadequate schools. Living in neighborhoods with high levels of poverty can restrict residents' access to quality education, healthcare, and employment opportunities, making it difficult for them to break out of the cycle of poverty.

Furthermore, public housing residents often face stigmatization and discrimination based on their housing status. Stereotypes and negative perceptions of public housing residents can lead to social exclusion and marginalization, affecting their self-esteem and overall well-being. Stigmatization can also impact residents' ability to secure employment or access resources, as they may face discrimination in the job market or when seeking services. This can further entrench their reliance on public assistance programs and perpetuate feelings of dependency on the system.

In addition to social challenges, public housing residents often experience a lack of resources and support services within their communities. Many public housing developments lack access to basic amenities such as grocery stores, healthcare facilities, and public transportation, making it difficult for residents to meet their daily needs. The absence of community resources can exacerbate feelings of isolation and limit residents' opportunities for social interaction and community engagement. Without adequate support services and infrastructure, residents may struggle to access educational and job training programs, further hindering their ability to improve their economic situation.

Moreover, public housing often fails to provide residents with opportunities for upward mobility and economic independence. Limited access to affordable housing in high-opportunity neighborhoods can constrain residents' ability to move to areas with better schools, job opportunities, and social networks. Without the option to relocate to more prosperous neighborhoods, public housing residents may remain trapped in areas with limited resources and higher levels of crime, perpetuating cycles of poverty and dependency across generations. The lack of mobility can also restrict residents' exposure to diverse experiences and perspectives, limiting their ability to broaden their horizons and pursue new opportunities.

Furthermore, public housing policies and practices can reinforce cycles of poverty by creating barriers to self-sufficiency and economic stability. Stringent eligibility requirements, limited support services, and bureaucratic hurdles can make it difficult for residents to access the resources they need to improve their circumstances. In some cases, public housing programs may discourage residents from seeking employment or increasing their income, as doing so could result in a loss of benefits or increased rent. This can create disincentives for residents to pursue economic opportunities and strive for financial independence, perpetuating a cycle of dependency on public assistance.

In order to address the challenges associated with public housing and break the cycle of poverty and dependency, policymakers and stakeholders must consider a holistic approach that addresses the root causes of poverty and promotes pathways to economic mobility. One key strategy is to promote mixed-income housing developments that encourage economic integration and provide residents with access to diverse opportunities and resources. By creating mixed-income communities, public housing residents can benefit from exposure to higher-income neighbors, better schools, and improved access to services and amenities. This can help reduce the isolation and concentration of poverty that often perpetuates cycles of disadvantage, offering residents a greater chance to improve their quality of life and economic prospects.

Furthermore, investing in community development and infrastructure improvements in public housing neighborhoods can help address the lack of resources and opportunities that residents often face. Initiatives such as building grocery stores, healthcare clinics, community centers, and public transportation options can enhance residents' quality of life and promote economic development within the community. By providing residents with access to essential services and amenities, policymakers can help break down barriers to social and economic mobility, empowering residents to build a better future for themselves and their families.

In addition, addressing the stigma and discrimination associated with public housing is crucial to promoting social inclusion and empowering residents to reach their full potential. Public awareness campaigns, community engagement initiatives, and anti-discrimination policies can help combat negative stereotypes and promote a more inclusive society. By challenging prejudices and promoting understanding, policymakers can create a more supportive environment for public housing residents, encouraging their participation in society and fostering a sense of belonging and dignity.

Moreover, public housing programs should be designed to support residents in achieving self-sufficiency and economic independence. This includes providing residents with access to education and job training programs, childcare services, and financial literacy resources to help them build skills and secure stable employment. By investing in residents' human capital and empowering them to pursue economic opportunities, policymakers can help break the cycle of dependency and poverty that often plagues public housing communities.

Furthermore, policymakers should review and reform public housing policies to ensure that they do not inadvertently perpetuate cycles of poverty and dependency. This includes revising eligibility requirements, rent structures, and benefit programs to promote economic self-sufficiency and incentivize residents to pursue employment and education opportunities. By creating a supportive and enabling environment for residents to thrive, policymakers can help break down systemic barriers and create pathways to economic mobility for public housing residents.

Ultimately, breaking the cycle of poverty and dependency in public housing requires a multi-faceted approach that addresses the social, economic, and structural challenges that residents face. By promoting economic integration, investing in community development, combating stigma and discrimination, and supporting residents in achieving self-sufficiency, policymakers can help create a more equitable and inclusive society where all individuals have the opportunity to reach their full potential. By working together to address the root causes of poverty and promote pathways to economic mobility, we can create a more just and prosperous future for all members of society.

Chapter 5

The Cycle of Displacement

Gentrification is a complex and multifaceted phenomenon that has garnered significant attention in recent years due to its profound impact on public housing residents and the broader community. In this chapter, we will delve into the intricate dynamics of gentrification, exploring its causes, effects, and implications for those living in public housing.

Understanding Gentrification:

At its core, gentrification refers to the process by which wealthier individuals and businesses move into a historically low-income neighborhood, leading to rising property values, displacement of long-term residents, and changes in the social fabric of the community. This influx of affluent residents often results in the renovation of buildings, the opening of upscale shops and restaurants, and an overall transformation of the neighborhood's character.

The Impact on Public Housing Residents:

Public housing residents are particularly vulnerable to the effects of gentrification. As property values soar and rents increase, long-time residents may find themselves unable to afford to remain in their homes. This displacement can have devastating consequences, disrupting social networks, uprooting families, and exacerbating economic inequality.

Moreover, the arrival of wealthier residents can lead to increased stigma and marginalization of public housing communities, further isolating residents and exacerbating feelings of alienation and exclusion. The loss of affordable housing options in gentrifying neighborhoods can also push low-income families further to the margins, forcing them to relocate to areas with fewer resources and opportunities.

The Cycle of Displacement:

Gentrification sets in motion a cycle of displacement that perpetuates inequality and undermines the social cohesion of affected communities. As affluent newcomers move in, property values rise, leading to higher rents and property taxes. This, in turn, forces long-time residents, including public housing residents, to seek alternative housing options, often in less desirable or more economically disadvantaged neighborhoods.

The displacement of public housing residents not only disrupts individual lives but also weakens the fabric of the community as a whole. As families are uprooted and dispersed, social ties are severed, community institutions are destabilized, and the sense of belonging and cohesion that once defined the neighborhood is eroded.

Addressing the Challenges

Addressing the challenges posed by gentrification requires a multi-faceted approach that combines policies to protect affordable housing, support vulnerable populations, and promote inclusive development strategies. Policy interventions such as rent control, affordable housing mandates, and community land trusts can help mitigate the impact of rising property values on low-income residents.

Furthermore, fostering community engagement and empowerment is essential to ensuring that the voices and needs of public housing residents are heard and respected in the process of neighborhood change. By involving residents in decision-making processes, advocating for their rights, and supporting community-led initiatives, policymakers can help build more equitable and inclusive neighborhoods that benefit all residents.

In conclusion, gentrification poses a significant challenge to public housing residents, threatening their housing security, social well-being, and sense of belonging. By understanding the dynamics of gentrification and its impact on vulnerable communities, we can work towards developing more equitable and inclusive approaches to urban development that prioritize the needs and rights of all residents. Only through collaborative efforts and a commitment to social justice can we ensure that the cycle of displacement is broken, and that neighborhoods remain vibrant, diverse, and inclusive spaces for all.

Case Studies Illustrating the Consequences of Displacement on Vulnerable Communities

Displacement resulting from gentrification and urban development projects can have profound and lasting consequences on vulnerable communities.

In this section, we will examine two case studies that highlight the impact of displacement on residents of public housing and low-income neighborhoods.

Case Study 1: The Mission District, San Francisco

The Mission District in San Francisco, California, is a historically Latino neighborhood that has undergone rapid gentrification in recent years. As property values have soared and new upscale developments have been built, long-time residents, including many low-income families and public housing residents, have been pushed out of the neighborhood.

One of the consequences of this displacement has been the loss of community cohesion and cultural identity. The Mission District has long been a vibrant hub of Latino culture, with local businesses, community centers, and cultural institutions serving as anchors for the neighborhood. As families are forced to leave due to rising rents and evictions, these social networks are disrupted, and the fabric of the community is frayed.

Moreover, the displacement of public housing residents has had a cascading effect on the neighborhood's social services and support systems. Families who are relocated to other areas may find themselves cut off from essential resources such as schools, healthcare facilities, and job opportunities, further exacerbating their vulnerability and isolation.

The case of the Mission District illustrates how gentrification can erode the social capital and resilience of vulnerable communities, displacing residents and weakening the bonds that hold neighborhoods together.

Case Study 2: Harlem, New York City

Harlem, a historic African American neighborhood in New York City, has also experienced significant gentrification and displacement in recent years. As property values have skyrocketed and new luxury developments have sprung up, many long-time residents, including public housing residents and low-income families, have been forced to leave their homes.

The consequences of displacement in Harlem have been far-reaching, affecting not only the residents who are directly impacted but also the broader community and its cultural heritage. Harlem has long been a center of African American culture and history, with landmarks such as the Apollo Theater and the Schomburg Center for Research in Black Culture symbolizing its rich legacy.

However, as gentrification has taken hold, these cultural institutions have come under threat, and the sense of community and identity that once defined Harlem is being eroded. Public housing residents, in particular, face challenges in accessing affordable housing options and maintaining their connections to the neighborhood's history and traditions.

The case of Harlem underscores the importance of preserving the cultural heritage and social fabric of vulnerable communities in the face of rapid urban development and gentrification. Without proactive measures to protect affordable housing and support marginalized populations, neighborhoods like Harlem risk losing their identity and vitality, with far-reaching implications for the residents who call them home.

These case studies offer a glimpse into the real-life consequences of displacement on vulnerable communities affected by gentrification and urban development. The stories of the Mission District in San Francisco and Harlem in New York City highlight the social, cultural, and economic impacts of displacement on public housing residents and low-income families, underscoring the need for policies and interventions that prioritize equity, inclusion, and community resilience.

By understanding the lived experiences of those impacted by displacement and listening to their voices and concerns, policymakers, urban planners, and community organizers can work towards developing more just and sustainable approaches to neighborhood change. Only through a concerted effort to address the root causes of displacement, protect affordable housing, and empower vulnerable communities can we create more equitable and inclusive cities that benefit all residents.

Addressing the Root Causes

To effectively combat displacement and its impacts on vulnerable communities, it is essential to address the root causes of gentrification and urban development pressures. These include factors such as rising property values, speculative real estate practices, lack of affordable housing options, and systemic inequalities that contribute to the marginalization of low-income residents.

Policies that aim to curb speculation, promote equitable development, and protect affordable housing can help mitigate the effects of displacement on vulnerable communities. For instance, implementing rent control measures, establishing affordable housing quotas in new developments, and supporting community land trusts can help ensure that low-income residents have access to stable and affordable housing options in rapidly changing neighborhoods.

Protecting Affordable Housing

Preserving and expanding affordable housing options is crucial to preventing displacement and promoting housing stability for vulnerable communities. By investing in the preservation of existing public housing units, creating new affordable housing developments, and providing rental assistance programs, policymakers can help ensure that low-income residents have access to safe, affordable housing in their communities.

Furthermore, supporting tenants' rights, enforcing anti-displacement policies, and providing legal assistance to residents facing eviction can help protect vulnerable populations from the threat of displacement and ensure that they can remain in their homes and neighborhoods.

Empowering Vulnerable Communities

Empowering vulnerable communities to advocate for their rights, participate in decision-making processes, and shape the future of their neighborhoods is essential to building more inclusive and resilient cities. Community organizing efforts, grassroots initiatives, and partnerships between residents, local organizations, and policymakers can help amplify the voices of those most affected by displacement and ensure that their needs and concerns are addressed in urban development plans.

By fostering community-led solutions, promoting equitable development practices, and prioritizing the well-being of vulnerable populations, we can create more just and sustainable cities that provide opportunities for all residents to thrive and prosper.

Displacement resulting from gentrification and urban development projects poses significant challenges to vulnerable communities, including public housing residents, low-income families, and marginalized populations. By examining case studies like the Mission District in San Francisco and Harlem in New York City, we can gain insights into the social, economic, and cultural impacts of displacement and the importance of protecting affordable housing, addressing root causes, and empowering communities to resist displacement and build more inclusive cities.

Through collaborative efforts, policy interventions, and community engagement, we can work towards creating neighborhoods that are diverse, vibrant, and resilient, where all residents have access to safe, affordable housing, economic opportunities, and social support networks. By centering equity, inclusion, and social justice in urban development practices, we can break the cycle of displacement and create cities that truly serve the needs of all residents, regardless of their income, background, or social status.

Chapter 6

The Education Gap

Education is widely recognized as a key determinant of an individual's quality of life, influencing their income, employment prospects, and overall well-being. In this chapter, we delve into the intricate relationship between education, income, and housing opportunities, focusing on the disparities that exist within our society. We explore how educational attainment impacts income levels and, subsequently, the housing options available to individuals. By understanding these connections, we can shed light on the challenges faced by those with limited educational opportunities and work towards creating a more equitable society.

Education and Income

Education serves as a crucial pathway to economic success. Individuals with higher levels of education tend to earn more than those with lower levels of educational attainment. This relationship between education and income is well-documented, with studies consistently showing that individuals with college degrees earn significantly more over their lifetimes than those with only a high school diploma.

Higher education opens doors to better-paying jobs, career advancement opportunities, and increased earning potential. As a result, those with higher levels of education are better equipped to afford housing in desirable neighborhoods, access quality healthcare, and provide for their families. In contrast, individuals with limited education often face barriers to economic mobility, leading to reduced income levels and limited housing options.

Income and Housing Opportunities

Income plays a critical role in determining the housing options available to individuals and families. Housing affordability is a pressing issue in many communities, with rising housing costs outpacing income growth for many households. Individuals with higher incomes have greater flexibility in choosing where to live, with access to a wider range of housing options that meet their preferences and needs.

Conversely, individuals with lower incomes often struggle to afford safe, stable housing in neighborhoods with quality schools, healthcare facilities, and other essential services. Limited income can force individuals to live in substandard housing, overcrowded conditions, or neighborhoods with high crime rates and limited opportunities for social and economic advancement.

Education, Income, and Housing Disparities

The connection between education, income, and housing opportunities underscores the disparities that exist within our society. Individuals from marginalized communities, including low-income households and communities of color, often face systemic barriers to accessing quality education, securing well-paying jobs, and affording safe housing. These disparities perpetuate cycles of poverty and inequality, limiting opportunities for social mobility and economic advancement.

Addressing the education gap is crucial for breaking this cycle of inequality. By investing in quality education for all individuals, regardless of their background or socioeconomic status, we can empower individuals to reach their full potential, secure higher-paying jobs, and access affordable housing options. Policies that promote equitable access to education, address income inequality, and expand affordable housing options can help bridge the education gap and create a more just and inclusive society.

Education plays a central role in shaping individuals' economic opportunities, income levels, and housing options. The relationship between education, income, and housing disparities highlights the complex challenges faced by individuals with limited educational opportunities. By addressing these disparities through targeted interventions, policy reforms, and investments in education and affordable housing, we can work towards creating a more equitable society where all individuals have the opportunity to thrive.

In conclusion, the education gap is a critical issue that warrants attention and action. By recognizing the importance of education in shaping individuals' life outcomes and addressing the systemic barriers that hinder educational attainment, we can pave the way for a more inclusive and equitable society where all individuals have the opportunity to succeed. Efforts to close the education gap must be accompanied by strategies to address income inequality and housing disparities, as these factors are interconnected and reinforce each other.

One key strategy to address the education gap is to invest in early childhood education programs that provide all children with a strong foundation for learning and future success. By ensuring that children from all backgrounds have access to high-quality early education, we can help level the playing field and reduce disparities in educational outcomes later in life. Additionally, expanding access to affordable higher education and vocational training programs can provide individuals with the skills and knowledge needed to secure well-paying jobs and access stable housing options.

In addition to investing in education, addressing income inequality is essential for reducing disparities in housing opportunities. Policies that promote fair wages, secure workers' rights, and provide social safety nets can help lift individuals out of poverty and enable them to afford safe and stable housing. Affordable housing initiatives, such as subsidized housing programs and rent control policies, can also play a vital role in ensuring that individuals with lower incomes have access to quality housing options.

Furthermore, efforts to promote inclusive and diverse communities can help break down barriers to housing access and create opportunities for individuals from all backgrounds to thrive. By fostering neighborhoods that are welcoming, safe, and supportive, we can create environments where all individuals have the opportunity to lead fulfilling lives and contribute to their communities.

In conclusion, the relationship between education, income, and housing opportunities is complex and multifaceted. Addressing the education gap requires a comprehensive approach that encompasses investments in education, efforts to reduce income inequality, and initiatives to expand affordable housing options. By working towards creating a more equitable society where all individuals have the opportunity to succeed, we can build a brighter future for generations to come.

Through collaboration, advocacy, and policy reforms, we can make meaningful progress in closing the education gap, reducing income inequality, and expanding housing opportunities for all individuals. By prioritizing investments in education, promoting economic equity, and ensuring access to affordable housing, we can create a more just and inclusive society where everyone has the chance to fulfill their potential and lead fulfilling lives. Together, we can work towards a future where education, income, and housing opportunities are accessible to all, regardless of background or circumstance.

Lack of education significantly exacerbates the challenges faced by low-income individuals in accessing affordable housing. Education is a crucial factor that influences an individual's economic stability, job prospects, income level, and overall quality of life. Therefore, the absence of sufficient education can perpetuate a cycle of poverty and hinder one's ability to secure decent and affordable housing.

Financial Constraints and Limited Opportunities

One of the primary ways in which lack of education exacerbates housing challenges for low-income individuals is through financial constraints and limited opportunities. Individuals with lower levels of education often struggle to secure well-paying jobs that provide stable incomes. This limited earning potential makes it difficult for them to afford the high costs associated with housing, such as rent, mortgage payments, utilities, and maintenance expenses. As a result, low-income individuals may be forced to live in substandard housing or overcrowded conditions, leading to increased health risks and reduced overall well-being.

Limited Access to Information and Resources

Education also plays a critical role in empowering individuals with the knowledge and skills needed to navigate the complex housing market. Low-income individuals with limited education may lack the necessary information about their housing rights, available resources, government assistance programs, and affordable housing options. This lack of awareness can make it challenging for them to make informed decisions about their housing situation and take advantage of opportunities to improve their living conditions.

Discrimination and Limited Housing Options

Low levels of education can also contribute to discrimination and limited housing options for low-income individuals. Studies have shown that individuals with lower levels of education are more likely to face discrimination in the housing market based on factors such as race, ethnicity, gender, and socioeconomic status. This discrimination can result in fewer housing options being available to low-income individuals, further limiting their ability to find safe, affordable, and suitable housing for themselves and their families.

Limited Advocacy and Negotiation Skills

Education equips individuals with critical thinking skills, problem-solving abilities, and effective communication skills that are essential for advocating for their housing rights and negotiating with landlords, property managers, and housing agencies. Low-income individuals with limited education may lack the confidence and skills needed to assert their rights, address housing issues, and negotiate for fair and affordable housing arrangements. This can leave them vulnerable to exploitation, eviction, and housing instability, further perpetuating the cycle of poverty and housing insecurity.

Limited Access to Stable Employment

Education is closely linked to employment opportunities and job stability. Individuals with higher levels of education are more likely to secure stable and well-paying jobs that provide the financial security needed to afford housing costs. In contrast, low-income individuals with limited education may struggle to find steady employment or may be limited to low-wage jobs with irregular hours, precarious contracts, and limited benefits. This lack of stable employment can make it difficult for them to maintain housing stability and may lead to periods of homelessness or housing insecurity.

In conclusion, lack of education significantly exacerbates the challenges faced by low-income individuals in accessing affordable housing. Education plays a crucial role in determining one's economic prospects, job opportunities, financial stability, and overall well-being. Low levels of education can limit individuals' earning potential, access to information and resources, housing options, advocacy and negotiation skills, and stable employment opportunities, all of which are essential for securing affordable and suitable housing. Addressing the educational needs of low-income individuals is essential for breaking the cycle of poverty, reducing housing inequality, and promoting housing stability and security for all members of society.

Chapter 7

The Role of Wealthy Investors

Wealthy investors play a significant role in the public housing market, influencing its dynamics and shaping the housing landscape for low- and middle-income individuals and families. In this chapter, we delve into the motivations that drive wealthy investors to participate in the public housing sector and explore the implications of their actions on housing affordability, availability, and quality.

Motivations of Wealthy Investors in the Public Housing Market:

Wealthy investors are drawn to the public housing market for a variety of reasons, each reflecting their unique perspectives, objectives, and strategies. One primary motivation is the potential for lucrative returns on investment. Public housing properties, especially in rapidly developing urban areas, can offer substantial rental income and capital appreciation opportunities. Wealthy investors often view these properties as valuable assets that can generate significant wealth over time.

Another motivation for wealthy investors in the public housing market is portfolio diversification. Real estate, particularly affordable housing, is considered a relatively stable investment option that can provide a hedge against market volatility and economic downturns. By including public housing properties in their investment portfolios, wealthy individuals can spread risk and enhance the overall resilience of their investment strategies.

Furthermore, some wealthy investors are driven by social impact considerations when investing in public housing. They recognize the critical role that affordable housing plays in addressing homelessness, poverty, and social inequality. By investing in public housing projects, these investors seek to contribute to the well-being of communities, promote sustainable development, and support initiatives that enhance housing accessibility for marginalized populations.

Implications of Wealthy Investors' Participation:

The involvement of wealthy investors in the public housing market has both positive and negative implications for housing stakeholders and society at large. On the positive side, their investments can inject much-needed capital into the sector, leading to the development of new affordable housing units, renovation of existing properties, and improvement of housing conditions for residents. This can help alleviate housing shortages, enhance living standards, and foster community revitalization.

However, the influx of wealthy investors into the public housing market can also have adverse effects, particularly on housing affordability and equity. As wealthy individuals acquire properties in desirable locations, they may drive up housing prices and rents, making it more challenging for low- and middle-income households to afford decent housing. This phenomenon, known as gentrification, can result in the displacement of long-term residents, loss of community cohesion, and widening socio-economic disparities.

Moreover, wealthy investors may prioritize profit maximization over social objectives, leading to the neglect of maintenance, inadequate tenant protections, and exploitation of vulnerable populations. This can undermine the quality of public housing, erode tenant rights, and perpetuate housing insecurity for marginalized groups.

Policy Implications and Recommendations:

To address the challenges posed by the involvement of wealthy investors in the public housing market, policymakers and stakeholders can consider a range of strategies to promote housing affordability, equity, and sustainability. These may include:

1. Implementing regulations and incentives to encourage responsible investment practices, such as affordable housing mandates, rent control measures, and tenant protections.

2. Promoting partnerships between public and private sectors to leverage resources and expertise for the development of inclusive housing solutions.

3. Supporting community-driven initiatives that empower residents, strengthen social cohesion, and preserve affordable housing options.

4. Enhancing transparency and accountability in the public housing sector through data collection,

monitoring mechanisms, and stakeholder engagement.

By adopting a comprehensive approach that balances the interests of investors, residents, and communities, policymakers can help ensure that the public housing market serves the needs of all stakeholders and contributes to sustainable urban development.

Furthermore, fostering a conducive environment for ethical and socially responsible investing in public housing can incentivize wealthy investors to align their financial objectives with broader societal goals. By promoting impact investing principles, such as environmental sustainability, social equity, and community development, policymakers can encourage investors to prioritize positive outcomes for residents and communities while generating financial returns.

In addition, investing in affordable housing initiatives, such as mixed-income developments, supportive housing programs, and community land trusts, can create diverse housing options that cater to a range of income levels and promote inclusive neighborhoods. By diversifying the housing stock and fostering mixed-use communities, policymakers can mitigate the negative effects of segregation, promote social integration, and enhance the overall quality of life for residents.

Collaboration between government agencies, non-profit organizations, developers, investors, and community members is essential to address the complex challenges facing the public housing market and create sustainable solutions that benefit all stakeholders. By fostering dialogue, sharing best practices, and mobilizing resources, stakeholders can work together to design innovative housing policies, financing mechanisms, and regulatory frameworks that promote housing affordability, accessibility, and quality.

The role of wealthy investors in the public housing market is multifaceted, reflecting a combination of financial, social, and strategic motivations. While their participation can bring valuable resources and expertise to the sector, it also poses challenges related to affordability, equity, and sustainability. By understanding the motivations of wealthy investors and their implications on housing dynamics, policymakers, stakeholders, and communities can develop proactive strategies to address these challenges and create a more inclusive and equitable housing landscape for all.

Through targeted policies, collaborative partnerships, and innovative approaches to housing development, it is possible to harness the potential of wealthy investors to advance social impact, promote housing affordability, and build resilient communities. By working together towards common goals and shared values, we can ensure that the public housing market serves as a catalyst for positive change, empowering individuals, strengthening neighborhoods, and fostering a more equitable society for generations to come.

Balancing Interests: How Investors' Interests May Conflict with the Needs of Low-Income Residents

In the realm of public housing, the interests of investors and the needs of low-income residents often intersect and sometimes clash, highlighting the complex dynamics at play in the housing market. This essay explores the potential conflicts that can arise between the priorities of investors seeking financial returns and the fundamental needs of low-income residents for affordable, safe, and stable housing.

Investors' Interests in Public Housing:

Investors in public housing, whether individuals, corporations, or institutional funds, are primarily motivated by financial considerations. They seek to generate returns on their investments through rental income, capital appreciation, and other financial mechanisms. Investors may view public housing properties as assets that can provide steady cash flow, diversify their portfolios, and hedge against market volatility.

Moreover, investors are driven by profit maximization and risk management. They aim to maximize returns on their investments while minimizing potential risks and uncertainties. This profit-driven approach can sometimes lead investors to prioritize short-term financial gains over long-term social impact or community benefits.

In addition, investors may seek to leverage their investments in public housing as a means to access tax benefits, government incentives, or other financial inducements. These incentives can influence investment decisions and shape the behavior of investors in the public housing market, sometimes at the expense of the needs and priorities of low-income residents.

Conflicts with the Needs of Low-Income Residents:

The interests of investors in public housing can conflict with the needs of low-income residents in several ways, creating challenges and tensions in the housing market:

1. Rent Increases: Investors may seek to maximize rental income by raising rents in public housing properties, which can make housing unaffordable for low-income residents. Rent hikes can lead to displacement, financial hardship, and housing insecurity for vulnerable populations, exacerbating poverty and inequality.

2. Lack of Maintenance: Investors focused on cost-cutting and profit maximization may neglect maintenance and repairs in public housing units, leading to deteriorating living conditions, health hazards, and safety risks for residents. Poorly maintained properties can undermine the well-being and quality of life of low-income tenants.

3. Displacement and Gentrification: Investors investing in public housing properties in gentrifying neighborhoods may contribute to the displacement of low-income residents as property values rise and rents increase. Gentrification can lead to the homogenization of communities, loss of affordable housing options, and social fragmentation, displacing long-term residents and eroding community cohesion.

4. Lack of Tenant Protections: Investors may prioritize their own interests over those of tenants, leading to inadequate tenant protections, limited recourse for grievances, and power imbalances in landlord-tenant relationships. Low-income residents may face challenges asserting their rights, addressing housing issues, and maintaining stable housing tenure.

5. Short-Term Profit Orientation: Investors focused on short-term financial gains may engage in speculative practices, such as flipping properties, increasing rents rapidly, or neglecting long-term sustainability considerations. This can result in volatility, insecurity, and instability in the housing market, affecting low-income residents disproportionately.

Addressing Conflicts and Finding Solutions:

To address the conflicts between investor's interests and the needs of low-income residents in public housing, stakeholders can consider a range of strategies and interventions:

1. Implementing Rent Control: Enacting rent control measures can help protect low-income residents from excessive rent increases, stabilize housing costs, and preserve affordable housing options in the face of rising property values and market pressures. Rent control policies can provide tenants with security, affordability, and predictability in housing expenses, ensuring that they can remain in their homes without fear of displacement due to rent hikes.

2. Affordable Housing Mandates: Requiring developers and investors to allocate a certain percentage of housing units in public housing projects for low- and moderate-income residents can ensure that affordable housing remains available and accessible in rapidly changing urban landscapes. Mandates can help promote social inclusion, diversity, and equitable access to housing opportunities for vulnerable populations.

3. Tenant Protections and Rights: Enhancing tenant protections, such as eviction prevention measures, lease security, habitability standards, and grievance mechanisms, can empower low-income residents to assert their rights, address housing issues, and maintain stable housing tenure. Strong tenant protections can help rebalance power dynamics in landlord-tenant relationships and promote housing stability for all residents.

4. Community Engagement and Participation: Encouraging community involvement in public housing planning, decision-making, and governance processes can ensure that the needs and perspectives of low-income residents are prioritized and integrated into housing policies and initiatives. Community-led initiatives, such as tenant associations, neighborhood councils, and participatory budgeting, can foster collaboration, accountability, and inclusivity in housing development.

5. Impact Investing and Social Responsibility: Promoting impact investing principles among investors in public housing can align financial objectives with social impact goals, encouraging investors to consider the broader implications of their investment decisions on low-income

communities. By integrating social responsibility, environmental sustainability, and community development into investment strategies, investors can contribute to positive outcomes for residents and neighborhoods while generating financial returns.

6. Collaboration and Partnerships: Facilitating partnerships between investors, developers, government agencies, non-profit organizations, and community stakeholders can leverage resources, expertise, and networks to address housing challenges, promote affordable housing solutions, and create sustainable communities. Collaborative approaches that bridge public and private interests can foster innovation, efficiency, and effectiveness in housing development and management.

The conflicts between investors' interests and the needs of low-income residents in public housing underscore the complexities and tensions inherent in the housing market. By recognizing these conflicts, stakeholders can develop strategies and interventions that balance the priorities of investors with the fundamental needs of low-income communities for affordable, safe, and stable housing.

Through targeted policies, tenant protections, community engagement, impact investing, and collaboration, it is possible to address the challenges posed by conflicting interests in public housing and create a more equitable, inclusive, and sustainable housing landscape for all residents. By working together towards common goals and shared values, stakeholders can foster a housing market that serves the interests of investors while prioritizing the well-being and rights of low-income individuals and families, ensuring that housing remains a fundamental human right for all.

Chapter 8

Breaking the Cycle

Breaking the Cycle: Proposing Solutions to Address Poverty and Dependency in Public Housing

Public housing plays a crucial role in providing shelter for low-income individuals and families. However, it often becomes a cycle of poverty and dependency for many residents due to various systemic issues. In this chapter, we will explore potential solutions to break this cycle and empower residents to achieve economic independence and improved well-being.

1. Education and Skill Development Programs

One key solution to breaking the cycle of poverty in public housing is to invest in education and skill development programs for residents. By providing access to quality education, vocational training, and career readiness programs, residents can acquire the skills and knowledge needed to secure stable employment and advance in their careers.

Partnering with local schools, community colleges, and businesses can help tailor these programs to meet the specific needs of residents and create pathways to economic self-sufficiency.

2. Financial Literacy and Asset Building

Empowering residents with financial literacy education and asset-building opportunities can help them make informed decisions about budgeting, saving, and investing in their future. Programs that offer financial counseling, access to affordable banking services, and incentives for saving can help residents build a strong financial foundation and break free from the cycle of poverty and dependency.

3. Affordable Housing Options

Expanding access to affordable housing options beyond traditional public housing can provide residents with greater choice and flexibility in their housing arrangements. Programs such as housing vouchers, rent assistance programs, and mixed-income developments can help residents transition to more stable and sustainable housing situations while maintaining a sense of community and support.

4. Supportive Services and Wraparound Programs

Implementing supportive services and wraparound programs within public housing communities can address the underlying social and health needs of residents. Services such as mental health counseling, substance abuse treatment, childcare assistance, and job placement services can help residents overcome barriers to stability and well-being. By taking a holistic approach to resident support, public housing agencies can empower residents to break the cycle of poverty and dependency.

5. Community Engagement and Empowerment

Fostering a sense of community engagement and empowerment among residents is essential to breaking the cycle of poverty in public housing. By involving residents in decision-making processes, promoting leadership development, and creating opportunities for civic participation, public housing agencies can empower residents to take ownership of their communities and drive positive change from within.

6. Collaboration and Partnership

Collaboration and partnership among various stakeholders, including government agencies, non-profit organizations, businesses, and residents themselves, are crucial to breaking the cycle of poverty in public housing. By working together to identify shared goals, leverage resources, and coordinate efforts, stakeholders can create a more comprehensive and sustainable approach to addressing poverty and dependency within public housing communities.

Breaking the cycle of poverty and dependency in public housing requires a multi-faceted approach that addresses the root causes of these issues and empowers residents to achieve economic independence and improved well-being. By investing in education, financial literacy, affordable housing options, supportive services, community engagement, and collaboration, public housing agencies can create a pathway to success for residents and break the cycle of poverty once and for all. Through strategic planning, innovative programs, and a commitment to equity and social justice, we can build a more inclusive and prosperous future for all residents of public housing.

Low-income individuals often face significant challenges in gaining wealth and agency in housing decisions due to economic constraints, limited access to resources, and systemic barriers. In this discussion, we will explore strategies aimed at empowering low-income individuals to build wealth, make informed housing decisions, and achieve greater control over their living situations.

1. Financial Education and Wealth Building

A crucial step in empowering low-income individuals to gain wealth and agency in housing decisions is providing access to financial education and resources that can help them build assets and improve their financial well-being. Financial literacy programs can teach individuals how to budget, save, invest, and manage debt effectively. Additionally, programs that promote asset building, such as matched savings accounts, homeownership assistance, and microfinance initiatives, can enable individuals to accumulate wealth and achieve greater financial stability over time.

2. Affordable Homeownership Programs

Homeownership is a key pathway to building wealth and stability for low-income individuals. Affordable homeownership programs, such as down payment assistance, low-interest mortgages, and homebuyer education courses, can make homeownership more accessible to individuals with limited financial resources. By supporting low-income individuals in purchasing their own homes, these programs can help them build equity, improve their financial standing, and gain greater control over their housing decisions.

3. Access to Affordable Housing Options

Ensuring access to affordable housing options is essential for empowering low-income individuals to make informed housing decisions and improve their living situations. Affordable housing programs, such as subsidized housing, housing vouchers, and rent assistance programs, can help individuals secure safe and stable housing at a cost they can afford. By expanding affordable housing options and addressing housing affordability challenges, low-income individuals can have more choices and agency in selecting housing that meets their needs.

4. Housing Counseling and Support Services

Providing housing counseling and support services to low-income individuals can empower them to navigate the complexities of the housing market, make informed decisions, and advocate for their housing rights. Housing counselors can offer guidance on rental agreements, lease negotiations, landlord-tenant disputes, and housing-related legal issues. Additionally, support services such as eviction prevention assistance, housing search assistance, and emergency housing resources can help individuals address immediate housing challenges and secure stable housing arrangements.

5. Community Land Trusts and Cooperative Housing Models

Community land trusts and cooperative housing models offer innovative approaches to empowering low-income individuals to gain wealth and agency in housing decisions. Community land trusts enable residents to collectively own and manage land, ensuring long-term affordability and community control over housing. Cooperative housing models, such as limited-equity cooperatives and mutual housing associations, allow residents to collectively own and govern their housing developments, fostering a sense of ownership, empowerment, and community engagement.

6. Advocacy and Policy Change

Advocacy and policy change are critical strategies for empowering low-income individuals to gain wealth and agency in housing decisions. By advocating for affordable housing policies, tenant protections, and equitable housing practices, individuals can work to address systemic barriers to housing access and affordability. Engaging in advocacy efforts, such as community organizing, policy advocacy, and grassroots campaigns, can empower low-income individuals to influence decision-making processes, shape housing policies, and advance housing justice initiatives that benefit their communities.

Empowering low-income individuals to gain wealth and agency in housing decisions requires a multi-faceted approach that addresses financial education, affordable homeownership, access to affordable housing options, housing counseling, community land trusts and cooperative housing models, as well as advocacy and policy change. By implementing these strategies, low-income individuals can build wealth, make informed housing decisions, and achieve greater control over their living situations.

In conclusion, empowering low-income individuals to gain wealth and agency in housing decisions is essential for promoting economic stability, housing security, and community well-being. By providing access to financial education, affordable homeownership programs, affordable housing options, housing counseling services, community land trusts, cooperative housing models, and advocating for policy change, we can create a more equitable and inclusive housing system that supports the needs and aspirations of all individuals, regardless of their income level.

Through collaborative efforts and a commitment to social justice, we can empower low-income individuals to achieve housing stability, build wealth, and shape their housing futures with confidence and dignity.

Chapter 9

Community Empowerment

In the realm of public housing, community empowerment plays a crucial role in shaping policies and practices that can lead to improved living conditions and overall well-being for residents. By highlighting successful community-driven initiatives, we can gain insight into the power of local engagement and collaboration in transforming public housing. This chapter focuses on showcasing examples of community empowerment in the context of public housing and underscores the significance of community involvement in driving positive change.

Successful Community-Driven Initiatives:

1. **Tenant Associations**: Tenant associations are grassroots organizations formed by residents of public housing developments to collectively address issues and advocate for improvements. These associations often engage in activities such as organizing community

events, providing support to residents in need, and liaising with housing authorities to address maintenance and safety concerns. An example of a successful tenant association initiative is the Bronx Community Vision in New York City, which transformed a neglected public housing development into a vibrant community through resident-led efforts in organizing clean-up campaigns, creating youth programs, and advocating for better living conditions.

2. **Community Gardens and Green Spaces**: Community gardens and green spaces in public housing developments have been shown to enhance the quality of life for residents by providing access to fresh produce, fostering a sense of community, and promoting environmental sustainability. Initiatives like the Atlanta Urban Gardens in Georgia have empowered residents to transform vacant lots into thriving community gardens, offering opportunities for social engagement, skill-building, and healthy living.

3. **Education and Skill-Building Programs**: Community-led education and skill-building

programs play a vital role in empowering residents with the knowledge and tools to improve their lives. Initiatives such as the Chicago Housing Authority's Education and Training Center provide residents with access to job training, academic support, and career development services, helping to break the cycle of poverty and empower individuals to build a better future for themselves and their families.

4. **Neighborhood Watch Programs**: Community-driven neighborhood watch programs have been effective in enhancing safety and security in public housing communities. By engaging residents in crime prevention efforts and fostering a sense of collective responsibility, these initiatives create safer environments for families to thrive. The success of programs like the Safe Streets Baltimore demonstrates the impact of community collaboration in reducing crime rates and improving the well-being of residents.

The Importance of Community Involvement in Shaping Housing Policies:

Representation and Advocacy: Community involvement ensures that the voices and perspectives of residents are heard and considered in the development of housing policies. By actively engaging with community members, policymakers can gain valuable insights into the needs and priorities of residents, leading to more inclusive and effective policy decisions.

Ownership and Empowerment: When communities are involved in shaping housing policies, residents feel a sense of ownership and empowerment over their living environments. This sense of agency can lead to increased civic engagement, improved social cohesion, and a greater commitment to maintaining and enhancing public housing facilities.

Innovative Solutions: Community-driven initiatives often yield innovative solutions to complex challenges in public housing. By harnessing the collective wisdom and creativity of residents, policymakers can tap into local knowledge and expertise to develop tailored interventions that address specific needs and improve outcomes for communities.

Sustainability and Resilience: Community involvement in shaping housing policies fosters sustainability and resilience by building strong social networks, fostering trust among residents, and promoting a culture of mutual support. These social capital assets enable communities to weather crises, adapt to changing circumstances, and thrive in the face of adversity.

Accountability and Transparency: Community involvement in housing policies promotes accountability and transparency in decision-making processes. By fostering open dialogue and collaboration between residents, policymakers, and housing authorities, communities can hold stakeholders accountable for their actions and ensure that resources are allocated effectively to meet the needs of residents.

Cultural Competence and Diversity: Communities are diverse and dynamic, with unique cultural backgrounds, traditions, and preferences. Involving residents in shaping housing policies ensures that interventions are culturally competent and responsive to the specific needs of different populations. By embracing diversity and inclusivity, policymakers can create more equitable and inclusive housing solutions that reflect the rich tapestry of community life.

Long-Term Impact and Sustainability: Community-driven initiatives have the potential to create lasting impact and sustainable change in public housing. By building strong community networks, fostering collaboration among stakeholders, and empowering residents to take ownership of their living environments, initiatives driven by community involvement are more likely to endure and yield positive outcomes over the long term.

Social Cohesion and Well-Being: Community involvement in shaping housing policies promotes social cohesion, trust, and well-being among residents. By fostering a sense of belonging and connectedness, community-driven initiatives create supportive environments where individuals can thrive, build relationships, and access resources that enhance their quality of life.

Community empowerment is a powerful force for positive change in public housing, as exemplified by successful community-driven initiatives that have improved living conditions, fostered social cohesion, and empowered residents to shape their own futures. By highlighting the importance of community involvement in shaping housing policies and practices, this chapter underscores the transformative impact of local engagement, collaboration, and advocacy in building more inclusive, sustainable, and thriving communities.

As we look to the future of public housing, it is essential to prioritize community empowerment as a cornerstone of policy development and implementation. By centering the voices and needs of residents, fostering collaboration among stakeholders, and investing in community-led initiatives, we can create housing solutions that are responsive, equitable, and sustainable for all. Through community empowerment, we can build stronger, more resilient communities where every individual has the opportunity to thrive and lead a fulfilling life.

Chapter 10

Policy Recommendations

In this chapter, we will delve into policy recommendations aimed at reforming public housing programs to make them more equitable. We will also explore how policymakers can address the root causes of housing inequality and wealth disparity. Housing inequality and wealth disparity are significant issues that impact individuals and communities across the globe. By implementing effective policies, governments can work towards creating fairer housing systems that provide access to safe, affordable housing for all.

1. Increase Funding for Public Housing Programs:

One of the most crucial steps in reforming public housing programs is to increase funding. Insufficient funding has been a significant barrier to providing quality public housing to those in need. By allocating more resources to public housing programs, policymakers can improve the quality of existing housing stock, construct new affordable units, and provide supportive services to residents. Additionally, increased funding can help address long waiting lists for public housing and reduce homelessness.

2. Implement Inclusive Zoning Policies:

Zoning policies play a significant role in shaping the distribution of housing in urban areas. In many cities, exclusionary zoning practices have perpetuated segregation and limited access to affordable housing in high-opportunity neighborhoods. Policymakers can address this issue by implementing inclusive zoning policies that promote the development of affordable housing in all neighborhoods. By requiring developers to include affordable units in new projects or providing incentives for affordable housing development, policymakers can create more diverse and inclusive communities.

3. Strengthen Tenant Protections:

Tenant protections are essential for ensuring that residents have stable housing and are not unfairly evicted or displaced. Policymakers can strengthen tenant protections by implementing rent control measures, prohibiting unjust evictions, and providing legal assistance to tenants facing eviction. Additionally, policymakers can establish programs to help low-income tenants access affordable housing and protect them from discrimination based on race, gender, or other factors.

4. Promote Homeownership Opportunities for Low-Income Families:

Homeownership is a crucial pathway to building wealth and financial stability. However, many low-income families face barriers to homeownership, including limited access to affordable mortgage options and down payment assistance.

Policymakers can promote homeownership opportunities for low-income families by expanding access to affordable mortgage products, providing down payment assistance, and offering financial education programs. By supporting low-income families in achieving homeownership, policymakers can help reduce wealth disparities and promote economic mobility.

5. Invest in Community Development:

Investing in community development is essential for creating vibrant, inclusive neighborhoods where residents can thrive. Policymakers can support community development efforts by investing in infrastructure improvements, supporting small businesses, and providing resources for community organizations. By empowering residents to take an active role in shaping their communities, policymakers can foster social cohesion and create environments where all residents feel safe and welcome.

6. Address Systemic Racism and Discrimination:

Systemic racism and discrimination have played a significant role in perpetuating housing inequality and wealth disparity. Policymakers must address these root causes by implementing policies that dismantle discriminatory practices and promote equity in housing. This includes enforcing fair housing laws, addressing historical injustices such as redlining and segregation, and promoting diversity and inclusion in housing policies and programs.

7. Improve Data Collection and Monitoring:

Effective policymaking requires accurate data to identify disparities, track progress, and evaluate the impact of policies. Policymakers should invest in improving data collection and monitoring systems to ensure that housing programs are meeting the needs of all residents. By collecting data on housing affordability, access to services, and housing conditions, policymakers can identify areas for improvement and allocate resources more effectively. Additionally, policymakers should prioritize collecting data on race, income, and other demographic factors to ensure that housing policies are equitable and address the needs of marginalized communities.

8. Foster Cross-Sector Collaboration:

Addressing housing inequality and wealth disparity requires a multi-faceted approach that involves collaboration across sectors. Policymakers should work with non-profit organizations, private developers, community groups, and other stakeholders to develop comprehensive solutions to housing challenges. By fostering cross-sector collaboration, policymakers can leverage resources, share expertise, and implement innovative solutions that address the root causes of housing inequality.

9. Support Sustainable and Affordable Housing Solutions:

Sustainable and affordable housing solutions are essential for promoting environmental sustainability, reducing housing costs, and addressing housing inequality. Policymakers can support sustainable housing solutions by promoting energy-efficient building practices, incentivizing green building certifications, and investing in renewable energy sources. Additionally, policymakers can support affordable housing solutions by expanding access to low-cost housing options, such as tiny homes, co-housing communities, and shared housing models.

10. Create Pathways to Economic Mobility:

Housing plays a critical role in shaping individuals' opportunities for economic mobility. Policymakers can create pathways to economic mobility by linking affordable housing programs with employment opportunities, education and training programs, and social services. By providing residents with the support they need to succeed, policymakers can help break the cycle of poverty and empower individuals to build a brighter future for themselves and their families.

In conclusion, addressing housing inequality and wealth disparity requires a comprehensive approach that addresses the root causes of these issues. By implementing the policy recommendations outlined in this chapter, policymakers can work towards creating more equitable housing systems that provide safe, affordable housing for all residents. Through increased funding, inclusive zoning policies, strengthened tenant protections, and investments in community development, policymakers can create vibrant, inclusive neighborhoods where all residents have the opportunity to thrive. By addressing systemic racism and discrimination, improving data collection and monitoring, fostering cross-sector collaboration, and supporting sustainable and affordable housing solutions, policymakers can build a more just and equitable housing system that promotes economic mobility.

Chapter 11

Building a Better Future

In envisioning a future where public housing serves as a platform for socioeconomic mobility, we must first recognize the critical role that affordable housing plays in shaping individuals' opportunities for success. Public housing, traditionally seen as a safety net for the most vulnerable members of society, has the potential to be transformed into a powerful tool for empowerment and wealth creation for all. By reimagining public housing as more than just a temporary solution to housing insecurity, we can lay the foundation for a more equitable and prosperous society.

At the heart of this vision is the belief that access to safe, affordable housing is a fundamental human right. Housing stability is not only a basic need but also a key determinant of one's overall well-being and prospects for the future. By ensuring that everyone has a place to call home, we can create a more inclusive society where individuals are better able to pursue their goals and aspirations.

One of the key pillars of building a better future through public housing is promoting socioeconomic mobility. Too often, individuals living in public housing face barriers to upward mobility, including limited access to quality education, healthcare, and job opportunities. By investing in public housing as a platform for socioeconomic advancement, we can break down these barriers and create pathways for residents to achieve their full potential.

Imagine a future where public housing developments are vibrant communities that offer residents access to high-quality education, healthcare, and job training programs. By integrating these services directly into public housing complexes, we can create a supportive environment where residents can thrive and succeed. This holistic approach to public housing not only benefits individual residents but also strengthens the fabric of the community as a whole.

Moreover, public housing can be a powerful tool for wealth creation. Historically, homeownership has been a primary means for individuals to build wealth and secure their financial future. By expanding access to homeownership opportunities within public housing programs, we can help low-income individuals and families accumulate assets and break the cycle of intergenerational poverty.

One innovative approach to promoting homeownership within public housing is through shared equity models. In a shared equity arrangement, residents have the opportunity to gradually build equity in their homes over time, with the support of public and private partners. This model not only provides residents with a pathway to homeownership but also ensures that they have a stake in the long-term success of their community.

In addition to promoting homeownership, public housing can also serve as a platform for entrepreneurship and small business development. By providing residents with access to business incubators, microloans, and mentorship programs, we can empower individuals to start and grow their own businesses. This not only creates economic opportunities for residents but also contributes to the overall vitality of the community.

Another key aspect of building a better future through public housing is fostering community engagement and empowerment. Too often, public housing residents are marginalized and excluded from decision-making processes that affect their lives. By creating opportunities for residents to participate in the governance of their communities and have a voice in shaping policies and programs, we can empower individuals to advocate for their own needs and priorities.

Community land trusts are one effective mechanism for promoting community ownership and empowerment within public housing developments. By establishing community land trusts, residents collectively own and manage the land on which their homes are located, ensuring long-term affordability and stability. This model not only empowers residents to take control of their housing destinies but also fosters a sense of community pride and cohesion.

In building a better future through public housing, it is essential to address the systemic inequities that have historically marginalized low-income communities and communities of color. Public housing policies and programs must be designed with a lens of equity and social justice to ensure that all individuals have equal access to opportunities for socioeconomic mobility and wealth creation.

One critical aspect of promoting equity within public housing is addressing the issue of housing segregation. Historically, public housing developments have been concentrated in low-income, minority neighborhoods, perpetuating patterns of segregation and isolation. By promoting mixed-income communities and deconcentrating poverty, we can create more diverse and inclusive environments where residents have access to a broader range of resources and opportunities.

Furthermore, public housing programs must prioritize anti-displacement strategies to protect residents from gentrification and ensure that they can remain in their communities as they improve and develop. Displacement due to rising housing costs and redevelopment projects can have devastating consequences for low-income residents, leading to the loss of social networks, community ties, and access to essential services. By implementing policies that prevent displacement and promote housing stability, we can create more inclusive and resilient communities for all.

Another key component of building a better future through public housing is investing in sustainable and resilient infrastructure. As climate change continues to pose significant challenges to communities around the world, it is essential to ensure that public housing developments are built to withstand environmental threats and minimize their carbon footprint. By incorporating green building practices, renewable energy sources, and resilient design features into public housing projects, we can create healthier, more environmentally sustainable communities for current and future generations.

Moreover, public housing can serve as a catalyst for economic development and revitalization in underserved neighborhoods. By strategically locating public housing developments in areas with limited access to amenities and services, we can help stimulate local economies, create jobs, and attract private investment. Public-private partnerships can play a crucial role in leveraging resources and expertise to maximize the impact of public housing investments and create thriving, mixed-use communities that benefit residents and the broader community.

In building a better future through public housing, it is essential to prioritize equity, inclusion, and community empowerment at every step of the process. By centering the voices and experiences of residents in decision-making processes, we can ensure that public housing programs are responsive to the needs and priorities of the communities they serve. Collaborative partnerships between government agencies, non-profit organizations, and community stakeholders are key to fostering innovation, sustainability, and resilience in public housing initiatives.

In conclusion, public housing has the potential to be a powerful platform for socioeconomic mobility, empowerment, and wealth creation for all. By reimagining public housing as more than just a safety net but as a pathway to a better future, we can create more equitable, inclusive, and resilient communities where all individuals have the opportunity to thrive and succeed. By investing in public housing as a cornerstone of a more just and sustainable society, we can build a better future for generations to come.

www.ingramcontent.com/pod-product-compliance
Lightning Source LLC
Chambersburg PA
CBHW070711250726
48662CB00001B/356